# BEING

*Guidance in how to BE
rather than how to DO*

By
Alicia Sedgwick

BEING rather than doing will slow the frenetic
stress of current daily life, bringing you calm,
peace and the ability to deeply connect

**Legal Publication Page**

This edition first published 2025.

Copyright ©2025 Alicia Sedgwick. All rights reserved.

Author: Alicia Sedgwick, The Communication Coach and Expert, www.aliciasedgwick.com

Editor: Wendy Yorke, WRITE.EDIT.PUBLISH, www.wendyyorke.com

**Publisher:** Serapis Bey, Arizona, USA

**Designer:** Natasa Ivancevic

**Front cover Image:** Photographer, Lily Frebourg

*Library of Congress Cataloging-in-Publication Data is Available:*

ISBN (paperback) 979-8-9925723-3-9
ISBN (Ebook) 979-8-9925723-4-6

All uncited quotations are the author's own.

# Dedications

This book is dedicated to Linda Mitchell and Emily Owen who inspired the concept of *BEING* at the start of the New Year 2025. Thank you, dear friends, for always sharing yourselves so openly and completely.

It is also dedicated to my beloved spouse, Annette, who is my reason for being.

# Acknowledgements

I am always grateful to my mum and dad, who live on in my heart and thoughts, and whose legacy I honour by writing this book, and living my life fully 'being'.

My spouse, Annette, who this book is dedicated to, because she is my *raison d'etre*.

Linda Mitchell and Emily Owen, who inspired the book, and continue to inspire me to remember to be and not to do, and who are so much of this book because they are love, authentic and kind.

Robert Mitchell, who was my brother's best friend, and has been a loving and supportive presence for my life. He is the husband of Linda, and father to Ems.

Wendy Yorke, my editor and author coach who guided me through my first book, and I knew would be the same caring, knowledgeable and encouraging person to turn to again. Indeed, she has been! I cannot express enough how she gets me, and I feel her with me - from her heart to mine - as I write.

My publisher Parul Agrawal at Serapis Bey Publishing, who I am so very grateful for and who has been with me since my first book. She always goes above and beyond to support me.

I thank P who contributed to the book, sharing her experience for Chapter 11: Being Well and Wellbeing. You sweet and gorgeous girl, I love you.

My 'brother from another mother,' my Jeffy, thank you for always bringing me laughter and joy and a happy release from any of life's cares and woes.

My dear family and friends who love me, care for me, support me and encourage me. I am so grateful to you all. You help me so much to be me and to always know the importance of being.

Finally, my students, young and older, you all have helped me to learn for which I am forever grateful. And I am proud of you all, cherished members of Team Alicia for always.

# International Praise For This Book

"Simply by being herself, through her gentle, reassuring voice, Alicia encourages us to initiate a quiet conversation with ourselves. In each chapter her candour and honesty empower us to reflect on our uniqueness. Layer-by-layer, she allows us to recognise the strength we all have, to overcome adversity and embrace life to the full. Her book is brimming with love, honesty, humility, tolerance and non-judgemental wisdom … marvellous." **Antony Lishak MBE, CEO, Holocaust Education Charity, educational consultant and author, UK**

"Alicia Sedgwick's book, *Being*, offers readers a serene and compassionate experience, akin to a gentle embrace from a wise friend. Its straightforward structure and thoughtfully titled chapters make it both accessible and elegant. The inclusion of song titles at the beginning and reflective quotes at the end adds a unique and personal touch. As a holistic stress management coach, I appreciate the emphasis on 'being' over 'doing,' encouraging readers to create space in their lives to disconnect from constant cognitive demands, such as their 'phones and social media and truly savour life.

I feel the book fully reflects this and the importance of slowing down before life passes us by, however tough that may sometimes be." **Gabrielle Françoise Achilleos, Integrative Nutrition Health coach, Monaco**

"This book is so beautifully written and has an amazing glow and structure to it. I love how positive the book is. Alicia's experiences and perspectives allow readers to reflect on their own lives and seamlessly integrate her tips and advice into their everyday. I love it. It lifts you up and fills you with confidence and positivity, a truly unique life-affirming book." **Phoebe Creed, (16) student, UK**

"I like this book because it comprises a step-by-step compendium of survival skills. Metaphorically, it enlivens the advice given to all air-flight passengers: 'Put your own oxygen mask on first'. At first, this sounds counter-intuitive. We are taught as children to think of others, to be kind and to be selfless. But Alicia Sedgwick maintains we can only achieve 'otherness' by making sure we are in good condition ourselves to begin with. In this short, but powerful book, she systematically outlines an interconnected set of life markers to help us sustain ourselves. She badges it, the call to 'being' rather than 'doing'. In this sense, it is a radical message. Her key message is that we are better, more effective and more personally fulfilled actors if we deny the often, overwhelming demands of market, work, family and numerous other obligations in favour of self-care. She provides key affirmations to do so. Her personal examples reflect the current political and economic circumstances that make her message increasingly essential. This is why the book is timely and valuable, and I will recommend this book to readers I know." **Karen Lane, senior lecturer, researcher in maternity services, teaching experience in theory, media and relationships, Deakin University, Australia**

"If you are seeking a template for peaceful, calm, meaningful living, *BEING* provides the recipe. Alicia Sedgwick delivers an authentic guide to living, born out of personal experience and written sagely. It is a guide for the young, a reminder for the mature and simply a message our current world is longing for. There is a purity and clarity of thought which kept me reading on even though, at first, it seemed too simple, perhaps naïve. Because of Alicia's dogged authenticity and openness, and love for the humans in her life, I noticed the themes begin to weave into a message that crescendos into a way of being that has the potential to elevate the human experience. This is exactly what the world needs in this moment. Thank you, Alicia." **Kathy Pickard, writer, retired teacher and University administrator, California, USA**

"This book is beautiful and faithful in its ability to inform both head and heart. One of the many smart things about Alicia's book is the song reference at the beginning of each chapter. The reference presented itself to me as an invitation into an immediate right-brain experience, just as I was preparing for some left-brain serious work. I love it!" **David A Leith, South Africa**

"What a joy this book was to read, truly wonderful! I loved Alicia's mention of music as a tool of transformation and the beauty and healing power that music provides us with. It was moving to learn of how Alicia talks us through her trials, similar to all of ours, her path in life has taken different turns and she was faced with many setbacks that she worked to overcome and challenge, coming back with even more fight; carrying with her a mission to guide others and arm them with tools and perspective shifts, building from self-belief. The way she expressed her experiences for other people to resonate with and take something from, as well as pulling the reader back into the reality and focus of each chapter is brilliant. The affirmations at the end of each chapter are a great addition too, fabulously freeing! She provides easy to understand tips and guidance, with many great takeaways for Team Alicia! Her teachings are simple, yet effective.

Chapter 2 especially helped me to look inward and reflect on a new perspective about relationships, revealing that what you accept within relationships with anyone will set and define the limits of your relationships. She reminded me of the importance of being bold with your boundaries and that setting boundaries is not selfish, nor boring. Alicia also discusses hard-hitting global issues, informing, bringing awareness and reminding us of the reality and horrors that are experienced by so many people; and that treating people with kindness is a positive step we all must take to make this world a more loving and accepting place. I also enjoyed hearing all the other stories shared throughout Alicia's book, which is insightful and an injection of hope. Her vulnerability throughout her writing is BE-autiful!" **Isabelle Kinsella, dancer, model and author of *Behind That Smile,* UK**

"Wonderfully written and full of positivity. I was having a very down day and after reading Alicia's second book, I felt optimistic and confident to face whatever life threw at me that day. We all need to have an Alicia in our lives and how very lucky and blessed that we have her." **Julia Creed, beauty therapist, UK**

# Being Alicia

Alicia Sedgwick is an English professional Communication Coach, Corporate Trainer, international bestselling author, speaker and Master of Ceremonies, based in the Principality of Monaco, with an extensive background in the entertainment and events industry.

She has been featured in international webinars, podcasts, blogs and e-zines from India to Australia, and from the US to Vietnam. Her communication and confidence-building training clients include corporate CEOs, non-profit associations, foundations and educational institutions. Her private training initiatives range from providing communication skills to international refugees from war zones and countries in conflict, to coaching seasoned executives in confrontational situations before key shareholder groups.

Her first book *Communicating Through Change* (2021) has been described as 'life-changing' and shows readers how to communicate through major changes in their lives. It is packed with real-life stories, practical exercises, insightful tips and uplifting affirmations. Addressing relevant challenges, which everyone meets at one time in their life, this book gives hope, resilience and clarity about how to move forward.

Alicia is known globally as The Communication Coach and Expert, and she leads Team Alicia, to help people to cope with and share their experiences of change, as well as to learn how to express themselves with confidence and power. Alicia has been through many unexpected and traumatic changes in her life, which she shares in her first book in intimate detail, to help people know that they are not alone and there are ways to embrace change and thrive.

She delivers training about soft skills development and communication skills for numerous private companies and non-profits. She has created public speaking and communication curriculum for the International University of Monaco and also teaches undergraduate and master's level students. She designs and executes public speaking training courses for the International School of Monaco, and she oversees their annual TEDx Youth Event.

Alicia has moderated international press conferences at the Olympics, hosted three TEDx conferences, and managed red carpets for the Laureus World Sports Awards. She has managed Talent Relations for the BBC Chelsea Flower Show in London, and in the Green Room of the World Music Awards.

A London city-trained lawyer, Alicia has worked as a professional mediator, specialised in conflict management. She was also co-founder and managing director of Absolutely Monte Carlo, an Event Management company, and Monte Carlo Media Inc. A professional blues singer and stage performer for more than 25 years, Alicia has hosted her own Internet Television Show and international Radio Show. She has a very high level of energy and is caring, motivating and inspiring.

# Contents List

Introduction

# BEING CREATED

At the beginning of the year, 2025, very dear friends, Linda and Ems, visited from England. As always, we shared wonderful, meaningful conversations, one of which took place in the sunshine on the terrace of *Fraise et Chocolat* in Roquebrune Village, in the South of France.

Ems asked us what our word for the year was.

Linda replied first.

"Gratitude."

I said that same word had come into my head, too.

Ems added her word next.

"Rest."

However, she did not feel comfortable with that because it did not truly reflect how she felt about the year ahead. She wanted to express not feeling compelled to be doing. I reminded her that we are not human DOings, but human BEings, and that led us to the word that truly resonated for us all – 'being'. Indeed, it inspired me to fill the opening page of my 2025 diary with all the 'being' that the year can bring, and every year thereafter. Including being grateful, bringing us back to Linda and my first thought on that sunny terrace in January. And being restful, to incorporate Ems' first thought, too.

This book has been written to help you as you go through the weeks and months ahead with simple lessons of being. As you read, enjoy being guided and supported.

You know from my first book, ***Communicating Through Change***, I am always here for you - #TeamAlicia for always. What does that mean? It means that when you are with me, and in my company, physically or when reading my books, or listening to my audio books, or watching my videos, you leave your cares, worries and anxieties outside the door. With me, you will not be judged. You will be supported and cared for. What happens in Team Alicia, stays in Team Alicia! You are free to be yourself without inhibition or fear. And it is that support, and care, and that freedom to be yourself that will always be here for you.

You will notice at the start of every chapter in this book there is a reference to a song. Music for me plays such an important role in my life. I was taught to sing from an early age, and it helped me to overcome my lack of confidence to sing in front of people. I spent many years turning my back on an audience because I could not face them to sing. But I find inspiration from songs which help me and my students to be free of self-consciousness. In my life, it is music that has been ever present. Sometimes when I go without hearing music and I come back to it, I think how did I survive without it! In this book, the song title and singer set the tone for the chapter and reinforces the message and theme. Sadly, legally I could not print lyrics without a lot of work to obtain permissions, but I hope that you will feel – or perhaps listen to - the music when you read the chapter and you will understand why that specific song is so important for me, and for you.

I remember, when I asked my vocal coach as a little girl, why I was so nervous to sing in front of people, and why I felt physically sick and was shaking when I contemplated performing as a solo vocalist. She said that singing was like standing in the middle of the street, naked and exposed, because you are giving of yourself completely, all vulnerable and bare. I always think of that explanation now when I teach and coach my students in their presentation skills. It helps me to support them when they feel so open and revealed. All the more reason for #TeamAlicia to protect and shield, but also to allow the transformation of being oneself freely and fabulously.

My theme tune for my coaching is Bruno Mars' song *24K Magic*, and it is the overall theme for *BEING* because when you can BE in every capacity I write of here, you are truly living the magic of your lives and giving the gift of wonderful YOU.

Chapter 1

# BEING CONFIDENT

*"I Have Confidence"*
*Sung by Julie Andrews*

We all have those moments of self-doubt and thoughts of not being worthy or of value. That we are going through our daily activities as an imposter not truly knowing what we are doing or how we are achieving what we are. Not having the belief in ourselves to speak up and express how we truly feel. Moments of lack of courage in our convictions because we are uncertain of ourselves.

I can recall vividly when I began my career as a lawyer many years ago in England, my self-doubts and total lack of confidence. I was fresh out of Law School and commenced my training with a law firm which I joined because it was created by the person I was articled to. I was truly thrown in at the deep end, having to work with clients in every aspect of the law. I had no trust in my ability, nor that I could be of any use and help to my clients.

This lack of self-belief, and that I was not up to the task or job, is nothing unusual. A survey by KPMG in 2020, *Advancing the Future of Women in Business*, for example, found that 75 per cent of 750 high-performing executive women who were one step away from being executive-level managers within a company, reported having personally experienced imposter syndrome at some point in their career.

This lack of confidence is not only associated with work. Think of all the times that you have wanted to ask someone out on a date or ask for a discount on a product that you so want to buy but cannot afford at exactly the price it is being sold for. Or when the food in the restaurant is not cooked the way you wanted it, but you do not have the courage to tell the waiter to take it back to the chef to cook the meat a little more.

On all of those occasions you do not believe in yourself to be able to speak up and face possible rejection. You do not feel that you are good enough. You worry about what people think of you, and because you are concerned that they do not understand how you are feeling with no idea of what you are doing, you cannot ask for help.

Let's go back to young Alicia, anxious, afraid and feeling totally out of her depth as a fresh new lawyer. Without confidence and insecure. What could she do? She had to build on the experience of success. She should have considered what she had achieved - written down the successful client outcomes - and reflected on them rather than the mistakes. Even, viewed the mistakes as a successful way of learning and growing. Instead of being afraid of facing the client and feeling that she had to know everything, and be everything, she had to realise that she could say, "I will get back to you about that." Giving her time to learn and develop her knowledge. Realising that sometimes we do not have the answers immediately. Knowing that when someone throws a ball at you, you do not have to catch it there and then. You can let it drop and pick it up when you feel able to do so.

Okay, so that building of confidence applied to my work situation. But you can apply the sentiment in all aspects of your lack of confidence.

YOU are unique. Even if you are an identical twin, you are still different and YOU are special.

Much of my coaching and teaching is about my students feeling confident and raising their self-esteem so they can speak in public. To be able to talk in a meeting, give a presentation, handle an interview, or tell their story. Senior executives, world leaders, young people, older people, all share the same lack of confidence when it comes to talking to groups, or even one person when they have to share themselves in some way. I give them the tools and techniques to overcome their fears and to make them effective when they speak.

I think about students from many years ago contacting me now and through the years telling me how their lives were changed because of my training and teaching. Why? Because it was about them knowing and putting into action the realisation that whenever you speak or communicate, you are always in control of your communication. I never know what you are going to say, so I never know if you have made a mistake, unless you highlight it by apologising or fumbling.

Being confident is realising that you are in control of your narrative and your story. It is exactly that – yours. As soon as you believe in the gift of you, and share that with your audience and the world, you can truly express yourself with power.

Indeed, your superpower is YOU! Every time you speak, or write, you are expressing your story, your take on events, your opinion and your beliefs. And I have the opportunity to learn from you, to get to know you and to grow with you. In those moments when you do not believe in yourself, I want you to step into your power - the power of YOU

Step into your light and shine brightly to act as a beacon of light for me, and everyone, to bask in.

Step into being fabulous YOU, and share that with me, and everyone.

In my first book, ***Communicating Through Change***, I ended each chapter with an Affirmation to help my readers literally affirm the guidance that I had given. The recommendation was to say these out loud to yourself every day. The response to this was very positive because it truly helped each person to help themselves with the knowledge shared.

So, here I go again to help YOU, dear member of Team Alicia.

Let's go back to the wonderful song title referenced at the start of this chapter, which contains a line that reminds you to trust in yourself.

**Being Confident Affirmations**

I trust myself.

I believe in me.

I am in control and in command.

I am confident.

I am being confident.

Chapter 2

# BEING TRUE TO YOURSELF

*"True to Yourself"*
*Sung by Olivia Newton-John*

It is essential in life to be clear about what is most important to you and live your life around those values.

What are your priorities?

What are your most important values and goals?

Can you think of times when you have done things to please other people? Not truly what you want to do, and you became resentful in the doing because you were not spending your time as you truly wanted?

I remember when I first met my beloved, I was running my own law firm, with my mum as my secretary and my dad as my accountant. It enabled me to go back and forth to the South of France to see and be with Annette. I could only do so with the support of my mum giving me the daily update about the work, fielding the calls, and passing on anything important to me. But I was also resentful of having to do that work and be in England, when I wanted to be with the love of my life. For me, I was not living my life as I truly wanted at that time.

However, I realised – with the help of some tough words from my amazing mum - that the obstacle I saw as taking me away from Annette, my work, was in fact enabling the development of our relationship. Without the freedom of having my own practice, I could not fly to the French Riviera every two or three weeks. Without mum and dad holding the fort and supporting me so considerably, I could not be away and could not sustain the essential work.

Therefore, I transformed my way of thinking and being. I reconsidered what I saw as an obstacle to being a way forward and progress. Rather than resisting it and fighting against it, I accepted it for how it was and the opportunity it gave me. I realised that I was living my life totally true to myself and prioritising my future with Annette and that I was able to do that in the present circumstances.

Imagine that your life is a bucket you have on the beach as a child and you fill that bucket with stones. If you fill it up with loads of tiny pebbles, which are all the unimportant things in your life, when you want to put the big stones in, the bucket is too full. You are not able to act on what is most important to you because your bucket, your life, your time, is taken up with all things that do not actually matter to you.

But you can fill that bucket of your life with the big stones first, and then if there is room, you can add the small, inconsequential ones after if you want. Your life and being true to you is about living in accordance with those big stones – your most important things. Whenever you say, "No" to something, you are saying, "Yes" to you and what your priorities are.

I have heard recently from several effective communicators that "No" is a full sentence. That really resonated with me because I believe that to be true to ourselves, we must know what our values are, and what is most important for us, so we can say, "Yes" to those and not feel that we are being selfish in doing that.

For example, the flight attendants advise you on a plane to put your oxygen mask on before placing it on your children or family or friend. It is the same principle I write of here – how can we be true to other people, if we are not true to ourselves?

This can also be described as setting healthy boundaries. Maybe, you feel resentful because you are being asked to do things time and time again, which is taking advantage of your good nature and goodwill.

Maybe you feel that you have to answer those emails for work long into the night and late after the office hours.

Those examples confirm that you are not setting healthy boundaries. If you do not establish with people how they treat you, and what is acceptable to you, and unacceptable, they will define the limits of your relationship, and you will feel under-valued and without control. You will sacrifice your needs, and the expectation will be that you will always say, "Yes" when really you want to say, "No."

Be clear about your time and how you spend it. In your work, with your team, make it clear from the start that you will work certain longer hours but when you are home with your family, that is family time. When you are on holiday, that you will not be looking at your emails and responding to them every day, if any day, when you are away. You are on holiday and not working.

Be clear about what you are prepared to do and not, from the start of any relationship, work or personal. When your values change because of changes in your life, communicate the changes for you and how that affects your relationship now. For example, when you began work and your career, you may have been happy to work long hours, weekends and holidays. However, now you are in a relationship, or a mother, and your priorities have changed. Let work know that you are happy now to do longer hours sometimes in the week, but that you cannot work weekends and holidays and every day working into the night. Then be consistent, stick to whatever it is you have set as your boundary. If that is not answering emails late at night, do not do so, or you are giving confusing, mixed messages.

Most of all, always know that you are not being selfish or weak when you set boundaries. You lose your power when you do not, and you lose your self-respect. When you say, "No", you create space for clarity, and you can make better decisions for yourself and everyone else.

Ask yourself, what is most important for me, my life and my way of being? And say these affirmations out loud to embed your priorities.

**Being True to Yourself Affirmations**

I prioritise myself.

I can say, "No", to say, "Yes" to me and my most important values.

I embrace my uniqueness.

I am true to myself.

I am being true to myself.

Chapter 3

# BEING IN THE MOMENT

*"Right Now"*
*Sung by Van Halen*

As you read this book, I wonder if you are seated still in your home, maybe lying in bed, or are you on a train or plane travelling to a destination for work or pleasure? Are you listening to the audio version, or watching the videos that accompany the book, as you run or walk in nature or around town?

I wonder if you are focused on the contents of the book and listening fully and attentively, or is your mind wandering, considering where you are going to, what you need to do next, or what happened earlier today before you picked up this book?

We are all guilty – at moments in our lives - of not being in the moment. Time disappears alarmingly fast and suddenly the day has gone. The evening has passed and if asked where that time went, can we honestly answer in meaningful activity and moments of pleasure?

For example, being on our 'phones and endlessly scrolling through mindless posts takes up so much time.

I realised recently that I spend an inordinate amount of time communicating! But I hear you say, "Alicia, you are a communication coach, so no wonder that you are doing that!" However, this is communication by messaging and liking and commenting on social media posts. I feel compelled to do this, rather than constructively spending my time doing what I really want to do and using my energy much more wisely.

With that realisation came a look at how I was spending my time and energy. Was I benefiting myself and my loved ones by not being with myself in stillness, and with them without my 'phone? Was I being in the moment of looking out of my window at the glorious view, or driving in my car truly listening to the music I love, or was I thinking all the time about everything else going on around me, or already in my head at my destination?

To be in the moment, I want you to consider the word, 'present.' That is what I did, and I realised the word has the following meaning. It is a gift. The 'present' is a precious gift. Being present and being in the moment is a present to you and all your loved ones, colleagues and friends.

Time goes by so quickly – you think that when you have an exam to sit, or a presentation to deliver – that it will be such a long time. How will you get through it? Your wedding day is a whole day and so it must be a long time? All these things fly by. They are not long at all. So, be in that moment, focused, attentive and mindful.

Comparing and obsessing will take you out of the moment. Even when the moment is one of pain or suffering, grief, or loss, accept that and be in it, knowing that by doing so, you will be able to let it go and let it be. That the moment will pass and you will be stronger for having acknowledged it and accepted it.

Do not think that you always have to be doing. You are achieving a lot by making the most of every precious moment by being in it. Not thinking ahead of it, before it, beyond it.

I recently spoke to a dear friend who mentioned that she always needed to be doing something when at home. That she could never sit still even when she had precious time with her daughters. I could relate to it. When I am home, I have always felt that I should be doing the washing, or emptying the dishwasher, or clearing a cupboard. Yes, things that need to be done at some point, but I could not relax into the moment of sitting with my beloved, and reading, or catching up on a television series. My friend was the same. I told her, as I told myself - just BE.

It is not easy for people like my friend and me, but it is essential to be able to make the most of the 'present,' that gift of precious time with our loved ones. Yes, the chores can be done, but set aside time for them, do them and then sit still and be in the moment of BEING and not doing.

As I write the chapters of this book, I am utterly engaged with the writing. Completely absorbed and in this moment. I am only thinking about the words I type, and the message I want to convey to help you as you read or listen. It is truly time in the present of this moment, this book. Not distracted by my 'phone, television, videos, or anything else. Precious present, indeed!

**Being in the Moment Affirmations**

I am present.

I am consciously being in this moment.

I am being in the moment.

I am now, in the moment.

# Chapter 4

# BEING BRAVE

*"Fight Song"*
*Sung by Rachel Platten*

I t is very hard to face the unknown without being fearful and afraid. Stepping out of our comfort zone is a big step, which is challenging and terrifying. What if you cannot cope? What if the situation is completely out of your control?

I remember when I worked in partnership with a 'friend' who was a lawyer, and after considerable pressure and long working hours to support him and the firm, he returned from a leave of absence to tell me that our partnership was over, and I was to return my keys to the office, my car and my telephone. All without any warning or real explanation. Though he did say that I would, "Thank him" one day for this experience!

However, because I thought he was a 'friend' I had no Partnership Agreement to protect me from this blow. It was just before Christmas and I was left with no work, no income, no access to my clients and nothing I could do to change all of that. Was I defeated? Was I incredibly angry with myself for not protecting myself? Was I completely without the rug from under my feet? Yes!

But … what was I to do? Give up many years of building a client base and developing a solid reputation as a lawyer? Change career and leave the legal profession? Give in to the defeat of all my efforts? No! I had to take back control of my life, as the song that introduces this chapter states.

I knew that I had to pick myself up from the feelings of hurt, despair, anger and hopelessness. I decided to set up my own law firm in the New Year from my home, with my mum as my secretary and my dad as my accountant, as I mentioned in an earlier chapter. What did I have to lose? I had lost everything before Christmas. What could be worse? No clients. No work. That was how it was … so … it could only get better!

In terms of being brave, facing the demons, facing the challenges, I asked myself that very question. What did I have to lose?

I think in asking that of yourselves when faced with the unknown, you can see whether there is too much risk involved, which you feel you cannot handle, or that it is worth taking that risk. I always say listen to your gut, to your instincts. They will tell you how you feel about that step forward, and if you can go for it, or not.

I answered that question by starting afresh on my own, and gradually my existing clients found me and new clients came to me. I was free to work on my terms, for myself, without being answerable to anyone – except my mum!

Being brave means moving forward despite uncertainty. It means that you choose to keep trying. It means that you embrace the unknown. You confront the uncertainty, and you make the choice to face what lies ahead.

You accept the unknown with the knowledge that you can respond to it in your way, and in your time.

*"You gain strength, courage and confidence by every experience in which you really stop to look fear in the face. The danger lies in refusing to face the fear, in not daring to come to grips with it."*
*Eleanor Roosevelt*

**Being Brave Affirmations**

What do I have to lose?

I am in control of my life.

I am in control of my feelings.

I am in control of my responses.

I am courageous.

I am strong.

I am brave.

I am being brave.

Chapter 5

# BEING KIND

*"Treat People With Kindness"*
*Sung by Harry Styles*

As I write this chapter, it is International Holocaust Remembrance Day. It is also the 80th anniversary of the liberation of the Auschwitz-Birkenau concentration camp. As Jona Laks one Holocaust survivor said after returning to the camp this year, *"It doesn't do any good for your heart, for your mind, for anything. But it's necessary. It's necessary for the world to know."*

There has been an increase in Antisemitic incidents in Europe since October 2023 with some Jewish community organisations reporting an increase of more than 400 per cent, according to a 2023 survey from the European Union Agency for Fundamental Rights (FRA). The report titled, *Jewish People's Experiences and Perceptions of Antisemitism* was their third online survey about discrimination and hate crimes against Jews in the European Union, taken between January and June 2023, from 8,000 Jews aged more than 16.

Also, there has been a surge in Islamophobic incidents across Europe, including arson, verbal and physical abuse and the targeting of mosques. All of which limits people's ability to live in safety and with dignity. But what have we learnt from the atrocities of the Holocaust? As few of the generation who lived through those horrors survive today, it is important that we remember their plight, so the future can hold peace and kindness.

I have the honour of working with the beneficiaries of Micro Rainbow, a non-profit organisation in England that run safe houses and socio-economic programmes for LGBTQI+ people fleeing persecution. My training is to help these people to be able to communicate effectively with confidence and raised self-esteem after they have suffered torture, trauma and pain. When they have had to leave their countries to face immense insecurity and continued anguish and vulnerability. I help them to express themselves and tell their story with control and command of all that horror and emotion that they have to relive in their Home Office interviews. This ability gives them back their dignity and the confidence to speak up and to communicate through the changes in their lives. To move forward into new jobs, and new relationships, and a new, stable life.

Those beneficiaries are people who were doctors, nurses, lawyers, dentists and other professionals in their own countries. They have had to flee, often without their children, to a country where again, they feel they could be targeted and abused. Without organisations like Micro Rainbow, where would these people be?

I recently had the privilege and pleasure to meet and work with Holocaust Educator, Antony Lishak MBE. He has developed *In Their Footsteps*, a new exhibition and educational resource using the ceramic footwear created by Jenny Stolzenberg from her exhibition of that footwear, which depicted the uniqueness of each victim of the Holocaust. The shoes that were taken off for the last time.

This exhibition enables understanding of the loss of millions of people who can no longer make their mark on the world and provides teaching for generations now to make their footprints and positive impact on the future. Resources are provided to help students create their own shoe exhibitions to be displayed for the wider school communities.

Antony has had a profound effect on my life. I relate to his workshops and message. The shoes are such a powerful representation of a life. They help us to realise that these were human beings, who had talents, potential, dreams and passions. So poignant, and so inspiring for the next generations to consider what shoes they will walk in. What footsteps will they take to ensure that by having empathy and understanding of the concentration camp victims, people will never again suffer such trauma and atrocity.

The powerful examples that I write of here are to demonstrate how kindness, empathy, understanding and tolerance are essential today so that horrors are not repeated and perpetuated. However, the acts of kindness that we can all make every day are not big, and they do not have to be on a global, significant level.

Being kind is having an understanding of someone who may seem to be different to you. It is giving that someone and everyone, respect and dignity. We may not be aware of what people are going through and we may not comprehend their way of being. What we can do is to be tolerant of their behaviour. Listen. Learn from them. Be gentle. Be open minded. Display humanity.

Being kind is also treating yourself with respect. Take care of yourself. Being gentle with yourself. Take time to comfort yourself. Listen to yourself.

Small acts of kindness lead to great kindness universally.

*"We must learn to focus on warm energy, always, soak our limbs in it, and become better lovers to the world, for if we can't learn to be kind to each other*

*how will we ever learn to be kind to the most*
*desperate parts of ourselves."*
*Rupi Kaur, The Sun and Her Flowers*

**Being Kind Affirmations**

I smile at a stranger.

I express gratitude to my family and friends for their life and light in my world.

I give encouragement to all.

I listen.

I see the good in you.

I see the good in myself.

I am kind.

I am being kind.

## Chapter 6

# BEING WELL AND WELLBEING

*"Just Fine"*
*Sung by Mary J Blige*

Around 15 years ago I was diagnosed with breast cancer. It was caught quickly, and I had the lump removed from my left breast, radiotherapy and medication for five years thereafter. I am checked every year and so far, all is well.

A few years later, I was in total agony and hospitalised for six weeks, while the doctors tried to discover the cause for the chronic and severe pain in my abdomen and back. It took them at least a couple of weeks and countless scans, tests and a lot of poking and prodding before they discovered that both my adrenal glands had died. It is a very unusual occurrence for both adrenals to die at the same time and never to be resurrected. At the same time, they discovered a lump under my left arm, which they took a biopsy from and discovered that I had a rare disease called Castleman's. Nothing to do with the adrenal failure. Nor was my extremely high blood pressure. Three different illnesses which had nothing to do with each other, happening at the same time!

It was no wonder that every day the doctors had given my beloved different reports about what could be the cause of my devastating pain and total wipe out. My poor Annette was told that: I had cancer; I did not have cancer; it was terminal; I was going to survive; and she was given a total lack of answers for quite some time.

However, within 10 days or so, the doctors were able to confirm the adrenal failure, the Castleman's disease, and high blood pressure and begin the treatment for all. While the hospital never discovered the cause of all the issues, my life was saved by the Princess Grace Hospital in Monaco. I will be forever grateful for everyone there and the team who took care of me and continue to do so to this day.

All of that took me out of the world for some months. My life became about rebuilding strength, and energy and managing the lack of cortisol in my body without the medication that keeps me alive. You know they say, 'Fight or flight' for when your adrenaline kicks in. Well, I do not produce that adrenaline anymore and I only have it in my body by taking tablets that contain it.

Thus, for me began the process of learning to live with a condition that could be a killer. Managing my medication to give me the energy to do my work, travel and all the things that I took for granted before this happened. Now, I could no longer, 'Burn the candle at both ends,' because I do not have enough candle to burn!

If you do not have health, you have nothing. My cancer diagnosis years ago and the subsequent severe illness I experienced taught me that. Being well is the single most important factor that we have in our lives. Not wealth, nor possessions because you can have all the money in the world and all the items or things that you can imagine, but if you are not well to be able to enjoy them, and you are ill and sick, they are worth nothing.

Being healthy and well is beyond important. Listen to your body and when it is crying out for rest, take the break. Stop! When you feel something is not functioning in your body as it has done, or it should do, consult a doctor, or nurse. Do not put it off. Take action to find answers.

Please, never push yourself and keep pushing. It will lead to burn out. Nothing is worth the collapse of your body and your mind. And let's turn to your wellbeing and your mental state. I would like to give an example here of a dear and wonderful girl who is the daughter of one of my dear and wonderful friends. Let's call her P here.

P experienced difficulty in grasping things and reaching the answers far slower than her fellow students at school, or in her extra curriculum activities. She felt that she was always behind, and she found school much harder than everyone else. She was frustrated and angry with herself, and she felt stupid and silly. She read and had to reread and reread because she forgot what she had read, and she could not understand what she had read. Her brain was like a sieve. In addition, when someone gave her instructions, she had to write them down or break them down or have them repeated a hundred times.

P thought that she could not be dyslexic because she was still in top sets at school, but she was deeply troubled by her feelings of frustration and stupidity. She thought that she needed to be tested for dyslexia, in case it was the cause of her problems.

Indeed, she was diagnosed as dyslexic and that, therefore, she processes things differently to other people without that condition. It was a relief for P knowing that she had a diagnosis and that there are resources to support the condition, and that she can now be given extra time in her exams and studies to give her the time she needs to process the questions. It makes a huge difference. She has felt a weight lifted from her shoulders and, in her words, that she is 'seen.'

P also shared with me recently that she feels proud of herself, now. She has achieved all she has in her young life despite the dyslexia, and she knows that she is not alone. She now has an explanation for her being different, and rather than viewing that as a disadvantage, she sees it as her superpower. She has had to work harder than everyone else to get to where she is, and where she will go, but she feels that this has made her a problem solver, and it makes her herself.

What I know for sure is that P is a remarkable young lady. I also know for sure that you, too, can be amazing and turn any anxiety, depression, frustration and anger to seek help, support, to have tests done to discover why you are feeling as you do, and to know that you are not alone. P can be your example, as well as mine, for being well mentally, as well as physically.

**Being Well and Wellbeing Affirmations**

I take care of myself.

I listen to my body and my mind.

I take action to ensure diagnosis and support when needed.

I focus on my wellbeing and alignment of my values and energy.

I do not push myself beyond my stamina and power.

I am well, with wellbeing.

I am being well, and have wellbeing.

Chapter 7

# BEING LOVED

*"I Wish You Love"*
*Sung by Nat King Cole*

For 50 years of my life, I was loved unconditionally by my mum and dad. They instilled in me a love of life, and to make the most of every precious moment, despite suffering tragedy and loss in our lives. My mum lost her husband, my biological dad, when he was 30, leaving her with my brother and I at only three years old and under one year old. Then, all of us lost my brother at age 18, when he was knocked down by a car at the top of our road, just before Christmas.

For nearly 30 years of my life, I have been loved and cherished by my perfect fit, my soul mate, and my incredible and amazing Annette. Long may that continue!

For all of my life I have had family and friends who support me, care for me and love me for who I am, and accept me for that. Long may that continue!

I have been loved, and I am being loved.

As the song title states, 'I wish you love'. First and foremost, I wish that you love yourself. I hope that you can take joy in every facet of your personality and your way of thinking. That you can feel comfortable in your skin and your body. That you can respect yourself and appreciate that we all have flaws, but those can teach us, and we can learn from them so we can be at peace with ourselves.

I have had clients when I was a lawyer and now as a communication coach, who are transgender. As a lawyer, one of my clients was a transgender woman; someone with a female gender identity and a male birth assigned sex. This woman had been married with children and her change of identity had lost her friends, family and her children. I have worked with both transgender women and men. They, too, have lost everything because of their gender identity.

Why do I mention these clients in this chapter about being loved? Their example of facing such antagonism, lack of empathy, understanding and consideration, has broken my heart. Seeing them broken and diminished has been beyond sad. Their total loss of self-esteem has been my challenge as their communication coach to raise it again for them, so they can express themselves with confidence and power as themselves.

For me, being loved means that you are accepted and valued for who you are. That you can feel seen, heard and understood. That you can receive support and encouragement. That you experience kindness, compassion and empathy. That you feel a sense of belonging and connection. No matter who you are, and where you come from, and where you go to, we all deserve to be loved in the way that I have defined being loved here.

I began this chapter by writing about the love of my parents and how that love was unconditional. Real and true love comes without condition. It has no limits. It is generous and non-judgemental. It is not ego and not vanity. It is not self-importance.

First, love yourself. Respect yourself. Be patient with yourself. Do not place conditions on yourself.

Then, you will connect to your world and the rest of the world and give healing to those who do not love themselves, or who have been judged and disrespected.

Being loved includes being loving and being vulnerable. It includes trust. It involves giving of yourself and letting down the walls you build around yourself because of fear of rejection and hurt.

> *"Tis better to have loved and lost than*
> *never to have loved at all."*
> *Alfred Tennyson*

Be affectionate. Communicate your love in the way you express that love. Do not hold back or hold yourself back.

*"Love is not something you do;*
*it is just the way you are."*
Sadhguru

## Being Loved Affirmations

I love myself.

I love without condition.

I respect myself and other people.

I accept myself and other people without judgement.

I am love and I love.

I am being loved.

I am being love.

Chapter 8

# BEING ACCEPTING

*"This is Me"*
*Sung by the Greatest Showman cast*

For those of you who do not know me, I am gay. I am Jewish. My birthday is September 15, and I am a Virgo. And I love chocolate cake! Now you may say, how can you love chocolate cake, Alicia, when carrot cake is so much better?!

Seriously, (chocolate cake is so much better!) what did you think when you read that first paragraph of this chapter? Did you focus on the 'gay,' or the 'Jewish' or the 'Virgo' and start to view me differently? Did you define me and label me by those terms?

How about if I say that I am kind, considerate, thoughtful, non-judgemental, open minded and caring? Do you think of me differently again? Or has the first paragraph stuck in your mind?

If I speak of people with disabilities, or disabled, or autistic, have you formed a picture in your mind? Or someone with cancer, or alopecia?

I am asking you to examine your levels of tolerance, and go beyond those to unconditionally allow people, situations and yourself to be as they are. It involves embracing differences and letting go of things you cannot control. This is being accepting.

Being confident, as I mentioned earlier, is essential, as is flexibility, patience, respect, sensitivity and thoughtfulness, to being accepting.

Merriam-Webster defines 'accepting' as: 'Able or willing to accept something or someone; inclined to regard something or someone with acceptance rather than with hostility or fear; tending to regard different types of people and ways of life with tolerance and acceptance.'

I suggest that it goes beyond that definition. That we should regard each other as equals. That we should accept people for who they are and who they are not.

Accepting others does not itself mean agreeing with them, approving of them, waiving your own rights, or downplaying their impact on you. You can still take appropriate actions to protect or support yourself or others. Or you can simply let people be. Either way, you accept the reality of the other person. You may not like it, you may not prefer it, you may feel sad or angry about it, but at a deeper level, you are at peace with it. And that is great!

When I teach public speaking and presentation skills, I refer to 4Ps. They include: Pitch; Pace; Pause; and Power. The tone of your voice; the speed at which you speak; remembering to breathe; and the power in the way you stand and use your body.

For being accepting, I invite you to consider the 4As, including: Acknowledge; Allow; Accommodate; and Appreciate.

When you experience loss or grief, the first step to moving through that is to **acknowledge** that you are grieving and going through the pain of the loss and the void caused by losing someone, or losing a job, or going through divorce and losing a spouse. Then, you can **allow** yourself to grieve and feel the pain. Cry, be angry and sit in quiet reflection about the person or thing that you have lost. Next, **accommodate** means that you open to the feelings, and you make room for them. You let them be in your lives. You do not fight against them. And, finally, you can **appreciate** the feelings because they help you and guide you through the grief, and enable you to communicate with other people, and learn what is necessary for yourself in the process. The sadness helps you to slow down and take time to soothe and heal.

These 4As can also be applied to being accepting of other people, as well as your own emotions, anxieties and fears. Think about that friend of yours arriving unannounced on your doorstep, who is lovely but quite a talker! And you had planned to be quiet and read a book that afternoon.

Firstly, you **acknowledge** their presence by saying hello and answer the door to them, **allowing** them into your home. Then, you **accommodate** them by taking them into your kitchen and giving them a cup of tea. Your friend proceeds to do as they usually do – talk, talk, talk. And you really are not listening. But then, you think about something that has been troubling you and you mention your concerns to your friend, and they help you work through it and resolve the issue. Your friend gives you valuable insights because of their experience and you can **appreciate** them.

Those 4As help us to be more accepting. But we also need to take our time when we react. Hasty judgements and quick assumptions are not the best way to reach understanding and find acceptance.

> *"God, grant me the serenity to accept the things*
> *I cannot change, the courage to change the things*
> *I can, and the wisdom to know the difference."*
> *Famous prayer attributed to Reinhold Niebuhr*

If you can let go of your need to control and become comfortable with the uncomfortable, you will be accepting and so much more at peace.

Change your perspective. You cannot change people or their personalities. What you can do is to get to know them and understand why they behave as they do. Why are they so loud, or gregarious? Why are they so shy or diffident? It will not change them, but it will allow you to appreciate them and accept them for who they are and know that they are so much more than these traits that they display.

After reading this chapter, which do you think is better, chocolate cake or carrot cake? The answer … is, of course, that a healthy debate about this is fabulous and being accepting of your choice, or mine!

## Being Accepting Affirmations

I accept and then I act.

I accept and appreciate my current situation.

I accept people as they are.

Every day, I learn to trust myself and the flow of life.

I let go of the need to control.

I am accepting.

I am being accepting.

Chapter 9

# BEING HAPPY

*"Happy"*
*Sung by Pharrell Williams*

Before my students deliver their first presentation to the group, or to me if they are an individual client, I like to play Pharrell Williams' song. I want my students to feel happy always when they are in Team Alicia. I also want them to feel happy when they present and speak.

For the most part, my students and clients are not happy when they public speak! Indeed, most of the majority of people rank fear of public speaking as number one – 75 per cent - according to the National Institute of Mental Health in America. Feared more than death itself. For some people, this means a fear of speaking to large groups. For others, it means speaking to a single person if that person has the power to evaluate you, such as a supervisor, interviewer, professor giving an oral exam, or your boss.

The term for the fear of public speaking is Glossophobia, which is derived from two Greek words: '*glossa*,' meaning tongue, and '*phobos*,' meaning fear or dread. In simpler terms, it is the anxiety or nervousness we can feel at the thought of speaking in front of other people.

One of my clients, let us call him Bob, came to me because despite delivering many presentations for his work, he still became panicked and anxious to such an extent that he could not get the words out of his mouth. He could not breathe or stop himself from shaking. Sadly, this fear and dread that he had in his professional life spilled out into his personal and social life. He shied away from social gatherings where he had to speak, and his self-esteem and confidence was at an all-time low. Bob was not happy.

However, as one of my students, we confronted his glossophobia. Gently, slowly and carefully, we tracked where it first stemmed from. Eventually, we found that the roots of his anxiety were deep in his past when he once presented and was ridiculed. As a young man, he was seen as different and artistic, which did not fit the image of his peers who were beer drinking, football playing males, unlike Bob who preferred reading and studying fashion. The voice of anxiety for Bob sounded like him being disliked and humiliated. For other students, the sound is that they will be laughed at, or they have nothing interesting to say, or "I am not good at this."

Later, Bob told me that the training was transformative, fostering resilience and self-assurance. It gave Bob confidence and self-belief and developed his communication skills which was invaluable for every aspect of his life. From expressing his ideas more clearly to being able to connect with other people more effectively, the benefits were profound.

We all need to face those voices, and sounds. Of course, they feel real and cause great stress and unhappiness. We need to answer those voices and quash them by considering the following.

Firstly, whenever you speak or present or communicate, it is never about you! It is about your audience, whether that be a large group, small group or only one person. It is about how you want them to feel, what you want them to think or do, as a result of your communication. Think about when you watch someone speak who is clearly nervous and uncomfortable, shaky and stumbling with their words, or mumbling and not looking at you in the eye. You think, *My goodness, this person clearly does not want to be here,* and as a result, you do not want to be there. That is not the effect you want to have when you communicate! So, if you are shy and nervous and anxious, the onus is off you. And I know that you are caring and considerate and you will want your audience to feel comfortable, engaged and involved with you.

Secondly, you need to rewire your brain. Instead of seeing the presentation or communication as something to dread, see it as an opportunity to share your knowledge and experience so your audience can learn from you. See it as an opportunity to share wonderful you. For other people to get to know you. The opportunity to share your message and your story. More than anything, feel excitement and happiness at the chance to connect with people and help them to feel happiness, too, by giving them the chance to belong.

In this chapter, I have focused on being happy when you communicate and present, but this context can be applied to all aspects of your life where you feel fear, dread, stress and anxiety. Once you realise that you are in control and command of the way you deal with situations, exactly as you are in control and command of your communications, you can let go of the worry. You can manage and channel your anxiety. You have choice always about how you respond and how you feel and what you do in response to feelings that arise inside you. You are 'response-able'.

Use positive visualisation for any situation where you feel uncomfortable and out of your depth. See yourself with a successful outcome. Picture yourself where you have a positive response to the situation. Breathe! We tend to forget to do that when panicked and stressed! Close your eyes and breathe in and out deeply three times, and on the third breath out, think of your happy place. You will be amazed at how you relax and smile when you do that.

When you experience overwhelming panic and find that you cannot breathe, focus on three things that you can see in that moment. Next, focus on two sounds that you can hear. And finally, move one part of your body. It will bring your heart rate down and you will be able to breathe again.

When you focus on the present moment and acknowledge your thoughts and feelings without judgement, you will be happy.

*"You cannot solve a problem with the*
*same mind that created it."*
*Albert Einstein*

**Being Happy Affirmations**

I focus on my message rather than my fear.

I release negative thoughts.

Every day I am happier and happier.

I choose being happy.

I am happy.

I am being happy.

Chapter 10

# BEING AUTHENTIC

*"I Am What I Am"*
*Sung by Gloria Gaynor*

I advise my clients and students that whenever they present, it is their Show Time! I tell them that all business is show business. This means that when you communicate, you are putting on an entertainment. However, this does not mean that you are not yourself and not authentic. When you put on an act and are not really being true, the audience will know that very quickly and your credibility will be lost.

This authenticity applies to all you do in life. You show up with honesty and sincerity. You have integrity and you stay true to yourself, despite pressure to conform to other peoples' beliefs and views.

Being authentic requires self-awareness and vulnerability. You express yourself with acknowledgement of your limitations, but at the same time, you will not talk yourself down. You never hide your emotions or struggles.

You will be able to let go of perfectionism. There is the safe knowledge that you do not need to worry about how other people perceive you because when you are authentic, you follow your passions and desires without concern of being judged.

When you are being authentic, you are not pretending to be someone that you are not. You do not have to impress others because you do not seek their approval. You do not compare yourself to other people.

I am sure that you have met someone in your life who was putting on a facade. You could tell that this person was not really engaged with the situation but maybe they wanted to please you and others in the group, and they went along with whatever was happening without their heart really being in it. Eventually, their commitment waned because they could not keep up the pretence. Or maybe you have been that person?

How is being authentic beneficial?

As mentioned in an earlier chapter about being true to yourself, when you are authentic, it leads to greater confidence and more satisfaction in your life. More fulfilment and success.

Being authentic leads to greater resilience and being able to face challenges with strength and positivity.

When you are being authentic, you foster trust and there is openness in your communication, which brings deeper connection with other people.

To be authentic, consider learning from your mistakes. Celebrate small victories and focus on your progress.

Engage and spend your time with people who you can be open with. Share your thoughts and feelings. A little at first, and then more as you build trust in your relationships. Slowly, share more significant experiences and your emotions.

And with all communication and in being authentic, practise listening. Truly listen to those people who you interact with, actively and empathetically. Seek to understand what they are saying and expressing, and their point of view, while never compromising your values and beliefs. Your conversations are not a competition, but a two-way interaction and an exchange of ideas and thoughts, which you give energy to and amplification. The exchange helps you to better accept and understand yourself, as well as the other person.

Being authentic, as all the 'Beings' written here, is a way of life. It is a process that will evolve as you grow and learn about yourself and the people you connect with. Trust and accept yourself and live in accordance with your core values. Embrace being vulnerable as part of your development. And know that when you are being authentic, you are shining brightly for us all to be warmed by your light.

## Being Authentic Affirmations

I am what I am.

I embrace my uniqueness.

I am proud of myself, and I stand always in my truth.

I let go of the need to please everyone.

I radiate positivity.

I am authentic.

I am being authentic.

Chapter 11

# BEING TOGETHER AND BEING CONNECTED

*"Reach Out and Touch (Somebody's Hand)"*
*Sung by Diana Ross*

I began this book by talking with my friends, Linda and Ems on the sunny terrace of *Fraise et Chocolat* in Roquebrune Village, Cap-Martin, France. We were together, we shared our thoughts, our lives and the sunshine. We spoke meaningfully and with laughter and joy. We also spoke - sometimes - with tears and sorrow. Always we spoke with openness and honesty because we honour each other's views and respect each other. All our time together was in love and peace.

I have shared so many such wonderful moments with loved ones in the same way over the years that I have been living in the South of France. And prior to that, in my hometown of Leigh-on-Sea, in Essex, England, although that was rarely in the sunshine!

Precious time spent with loved ones and being together is one of the greatest gifts of life. When you connect with those people you love and have their understanding of your heart as if they carry it in their bodies, it is special beyond words.

Connect with those people you care about and your community. They say that, 'No man is an island', and indeed, if we have the chance to be part of a community and be with people of like mind and values, then that opportunity for being together is one to be seized on and cherished.

Being together with friends and family is beautiful. If you are with someone or people who make you feel safe, and understood, you realise that you are not alone. When you share your experience and experiences and your adventures, it brings joy and also, fun.

Being together with people who appreciate you, and love you for all you are, flaws and all, gives you the encouragement to flourish.

When I spoke to my beloved about this chapter, she said that being together is not about being joined at the hip! Rather that when you are with anyone, a partner, a friend, a spouse, a lover, that you always retain your individuality and your independence. That you experience the great variety of life and possibilities together, and apart, so you can both grow and develop yourselves and share all of yourself with each other.

Old friends are a profound part of our lives, and the experiences shared with them are significant to our life. The people who have been together with me since I was a child and have known me through all the changes in my life, are so important to me. With them, I do not have to explain myself. They know how I was with my parents, and they knew my parents and my brother, and they know the influence of them in my life and the effect of their loss for me, and for these family and friends.

However, never be afraid to connect with different people over the years. This will enrich your life. I like the idea that friends are like flowers. You grow them in different soil – some to laugh with, some to debate with, some to play with, and do sports together and some to expand your spirituality. In the different shared experiences, the friendship will blossom. But do not be afeared when the flower does not bloom on an occasion because there are seasons for friends, like the time of a flower. Allow your connections to ebb and flow and nurture them always not out of obligation and duty, but through mutual reward and fun.

Sometimes to truly connect, we have to disconnect. For example, social media can take so much of our energy, concentration and focus. And in that time, while we are connecting with our friends and family, business colleagues and acquaintances, it is draining us of the direct and personal contact that feeds us and energises us.

When you step back from social media, and put your 'phones down for an evening, or a day, or a few days, it gives you the recharge that is necessary for you to be together with yourself, and those people you love or are associated with. Sometimes, disconnecting allows you to have a detox of all that massive information in your head, so you can connect to all the new ideas and inspiration and learn new things about yourself and your relationships.

We live in a world that is very isolationist, and we are isolated. We no longer have big communities to support and nourish us. So much of life is lived in small worlds – on our screens. Reduced personal and direct contact. It brings me to this; being together and developing a community is an important part of being. Wherever you can and whenever you can, bring people together. I speak of Team Alicia, a community I developed through my coaching, teaching and training. It is a place for people to belong, where they can be themselves without fear and inhibition.

Think of all the communities you belong to now and can develop in the future. Bring people together for mutual support, learning, care, consideration and empowerment. If you reach out to one person, extend your hand of friendship and think of the togetherness that will be fostered in the world.

## Being Together and Being Connected Affirmations

I foster positive and loving relationships.

I am worthy of deep meaningful connections.

I create space for meaningful relationships in my life.

I am open to new, positive connections in my life.

I am grateful for the love and togetherness I have in my life.

I am connected.

I am being connected.

Chapter 12

# BEING FORGIVING

*"Forgiveness"*
*Sung by Jason Upton*

One of the fabulous things about being a teacher is that I learn so much from my students. Every person who I coach, and train has a different perspective and a different story. I am honoured to share that with them, as they learn and grow with me.

A student, who I will call R, came to my training with a need for confidence boosting and raising of her self-esteem. During the first group sessions, she had introduced herself and said she was going to bake me a chocolate cake to her very own recipe because she had been an owner of a *Pâtisserie*. She had my attention from the start! However, it was in the one-to-one sessions after group meetings where I really came to know her.

R shared with me that she had been in an abusive and controlling relationship, which had led her to alcohol and drug abuse. She had been in a downward spiral that culminated in her husband taking their two children from her and leaving her destitute and homeless. She had lost everything. R realised from this totally low point in her life that she had to be clean. She had to sober up and kick the drug habit. She ended up in prison at one point, but from there managed to get into a rehab programme, and very slowly she started to rebuild herself and her life.

She managed to find accommodation and a safe place to live, and she found work to give her back some dignity. By the time she came to my training, she was sober, clean and starting the process to apply for contact with her children. She was truly strong and facing her demons, as well as confronting the bully who had destroyed her life through a legal process.

What struck me the most about R was not only her courage and resilience, but her view of her x-husband, and her abuser. R told me that she forgave him. She did not see herself as a victim. She saw him as giving her fortitude, strength and the chance to reclaim her identity and be a better person for that.

R took the view that by letting go of her anger, fear and suffering at the hands of her abuser, she could take back control of herself and her life. And in forgiving him and herself, she could also be free of the pain.

Living without bitterness and lack of hope, gave R the ability to move on and take herself out of the depths of despair, to shine her bright light once again. What a privilege it was for me to be part of her growth back to a brighter reality through the coaching I shared with her to regain and raise her self-esteem, confidence and ability to express herself with impact and effectively. Also, having had the legal background in my earlier life as a lawyer, I was able to hold her hand through the legal process, so she could see her children again. Standing by her side, at least metaphorically if not actually, was an honour. And I started to see R thrive.

I write of this without going too deeply into R's experience and horror because I wanted to give you an idea of how being forgiving is … in reality. R went through hate, anger, hurt and hit rock bottom. She chose to let go of the resentment, and hostility, to feel compassion not only for her abuser, but even more importantly, for herself. She saw that by being forgiving she was not weak, but rather she was being released from the weight of the burdens her x had put on her, so she was at peace, or at least strong enough to battle for her rights.

In the process that R went through, she had to forgive herself. As long as she held guilt and blame, she could not move forward. It was essential for R not to judge herself harshly and to be able to understand why she responded as she did, and how she could control those negative acts so as not to destroy her ever again.

Also, R gave me valuable lessons. I had been abused as a child by an uncle. That left its mark on me and my attitude to men, my distrust and vulnerability. It took me a very long time to speak about it, let alone write about it in my first book. But in understanding that I could let the pain and shame go by forgiving my uncle and myself, I could be profoundly at peace.

As with everything, being forgiving is a process. If you commit to treating yourself and other people with compassion, respect and empathy, the forgiveness will come. Do not make excuses for your behaviour or that of others, but acknowledge, learn, repair and heal and let go of the negative. In the letting go, you can let yourself live peacefully and wholly.

Being forgiving is not a substitute for being accountable. It is to maintain your self-respect. You do not have to reconcile with anyone who you choose to forgive, but you are free of them if you forgive them. As with yourself, forgive yourself as R did. She took her forgiveness to make amends, improve herself and her utmost not to repeat the mistakes.

I am not a religious person, but a part of the Lord's Prayer in the Bible, Matthew 6: 9-13, sums up all I am writing in this chapter.

*"And forgive us our trespasses, as we forgive*
*those who trespass against us."*
*The Bible*

## Being Forgiving Affirmations

Forgiveness is empowering.

I let go of the past to move forward.

I forgive to set myself free.

I forgive other people as I forgive myself, one day at a time, with sincerity and loving compassion.

I am forgiving.

I am being forgiving.

## Chapter 13

# BEING PLAYFUL

*"Girls Just Want to Have Fun"*
*Sung by Cyndi Lauper*

Maybe you have a photograph of yourself as a child, or a photo of your children in view somewhere in your home. Seeing that picture reminds you that you were playful and so are your children. It reminds you that you like to have fun and not take life too seriously. That you want to bring enjoyment to your life and your relationships.

I am blessed to have a cousin who has always been more like a brother to me after I lost my wonderful brother, Leslie. Whenever I saw Jeff as a child, I was so happy. Being with him was an escape from any of the worries of my life, and all my fears and anxieties. Maybe the girls at school had been bullying me, or taking sides against me, and I did not feel that I fitted in. None of that was in my mind when I played with Jeff, and we jumped over bamboo sticks in the garden, or went into the woods as explorers and pretended to be Robin Hood.

We laughed so hard that my tummy hurt, and I cried with tears of laughter.

The wonderful thing is that whenever I see Jeff now, or speak with him, I have the same feelings of getting away from any stress or strain. We can still be childlike in our optimism, encouragement and support, and with the understanding of each other and deep love. We still laugh and think of silly ways of having fun and avoiding responsibilities and cares. With him I am transported to the feelings of lightness and being playful.

I also have a dear friend who sends silly jokes, which are uplifting. Sometimes if he is going through sad times or challenges, he sends a lot of the jokes, and I know that he needs the release and relief. He makes me laugh and I am aware that when he shares the jokes, he is making himself feel better, too. For me, that makes the receiving of them even more valued and cherished.

As children, we are innocent, curious and funny. We can dance, sing, play games and we expect nothing and find joy in such small activities. I remember how I loved riding my bike and cycling to the newsagent round the corner and filling my saddle bag with chocolate bars and sweets. Everything was done with abandon, fearlessness and comfort. And so why, as we grow older and become adults do we lose that ability to play freely and without concern of what people will think of us?

There have been many studies which demonstrate that playfulness in adulthood is not only beneficial for our physical and mental health, but also necessary for us to function at our best.

Think of all the ways that you can bring playfulness into your adult life. My friend shares jokes. You could do the same with friends or even co-workers. Try a new board game with loved ones. I love playing board games, such as Scrabble, or playing cards with my friends and my beloved. They are such fun, and the game engrosses me in that precious moment.

Sing, dance, dress up in silly costumes, create a Zen Garden and do spontaneous things with your loved one, take time for each other and make the moment playful. Being unstructured in your usually busy, structured week.

There is the old saying that, 'Laughter is the best medicine', and I truly believe that to be the case. I always say that I am at my funniest when most sick or ill. Being able to laugh, especially at yourself, is freeing and liberating.

Being playful will remind you not to be bothered about what people think of you. It reminds you to be yourself. It reminds you that there is relief in this difficult world, and you can step away from all the seriousness. It reminds you that you can be creative, healed and bring joy to your relationships.

*"Laughter, song and dance create emotional*
*and spiritual connection.*
*They remind us of the one thing that truly matters*
*when we are searching for comfort, celebration,*
*inspiration, or healing; we are not alone."*
*Brené Brown*

## Being Playful Affirmations

I give myself time to have fun.

I can be silly, and I love being that way.

I cherish every moment shared in laughter and joy.

I am thankful for my ability to have fun.

I attract laughter and joy, like a magnet making the world a brighter place.

I am playful.

I am being playful.

Chapter 14

# BEING STILL

*"Be Still"*
*Sung by Travis Greene*

I began this book by telling you where it all started with our words for the year, and you will recall that Ems original word was, "Rest." But it did not reflect what she truly wanted to achieve during the year. That is why I am writing this chapter, because I believe that being still was a more accurate description of how Ems wanted to be.

Being still is being at rest, and it is also being serene, quiet, tranquil, calm and untroubled. It means that we are not striving or feeling compelled to do and move or be active. We can be at peace, letting all stress go and releasing anxiety, fear and the commotion that exists in our minds when we are overwhelmed and exhausted.

I always wanted to be serene! I looked at actresses like Grace Kelly and they seemed to have this air of elegance, calm and peacefulness. No lines on their faces that showed agitation and strain. Oh, to radiate that quiet power. It is ironic that in Monaco, Princess Grace was known as Her Serene Highness!

As I have become older, I still desire that serenity, but I now understand that it comes from the ability to be still, and to create moments of inactivity, quiet and peace. Some people achieve this state in meditation because it gives a focus on quietening the mind and deep relaxation. Personally, I have never been able to master the art of meditation, but I find the stillness in being beside the sea, hearing the lap of the waves on the shore, or being seated with my face directed to the sun.

For the benefit of being still, we need to spend some moments with ourselves. Not being alone but being in solitude. In that moment, we can listen to our intuition and obtain answers to any issues that trouble us. If we are constantly on the move, hustling and bustling, we cannot hear those valuable insights, which our gut gives us.

When you are being still, the world can spin around you. It allows you to focus on this noisy world we live in. Stillness is in your control when all else is spiralling around you. Keep cool. Be patient. Breathe. Do not rush into a decision or be pressured to do so. If your mind is in a constant state of agitation, or you are occupied by mindless distractions, you cannot bring stillness to your life, and it will lead you to being fraught and frazzled.

I wonder if you ever think about your day and how you spend it? Are you mostly rushing around, constantly reading and answering messages, talking, always connected if not by your 'phones, then watching television, and checking on the news, and ticking off tasks from your list like a machine? I get it! I have done the same. But I now know and realise that less movement, less doing, less rushing, brings peace, better health, and so much more joy. Being still is to be savoured.

Each day, try to sit still for a moment. And each day add to that sitting still for longer. Then, try to do less each day. Once again, breathe. Slow down. Be in the moment and enjoy that rather than always searching for joy. Refuel and replenish yourself in the moment of stillness.

We seem to feel that if we are not doing and we stop, and we rest, that this is lazy and unproductive, that taking care of ourselves is selfish. So, we must keep active and keep going. But if we take time for stillness, it is so much more effective for being able to continue to help other people and help ourselves.

However, you need to take rest and be still. Do it! Take a break from technology for a day, or more, if you can. Take a hot bath. Go for a walk. Spend time with a loved one. Exercise. What makes you feel rested is unique to you. Honour yourself by being still in the way that you need to and can do.

Plan for the stillness. In your busy week, schedule that time for being still and resting. Plan the time you need to restore and replenish your mind and body. Remove yourself from daily responsibilities and distractions, so you can consider new perspectives and a renewal of your mind. For even a few minutes a day, spend time being and not doing.

*"Learning how to be still, to really be still, and let*
*life happen – that stillness becomes a radiance."*
*Morgan Freeman*

If you need to be doing, make that doing commitment to being still.

## Being Still Affirmations

I am still and quiet, giving me peace and serenity.

I breathe in strength, and I breathe out calm.

My power is in the present moment.

I am still.

I am being still.

Chapter 15

# BEING HOPEFUL

*"Don't Stop Believing"*
*Sung by Journey*

I have always been an optimistic person. Even through tragedy and trauma, I see that there is light at the end of the tunnel, and that light is not the headlights of a train hurtling towards me!

Being hopeful for me is to have the belief that you can shape your life, and you are motivated to reach goals. No matter what the outcome, you have learned from the journey and experience, and it will give you positive results.

If you are hopeful, you accept change rather than be fearful of it because you feel always that it is leading you to the next steps and circumstances, which will be better and more fulfilling. In addition, you embrace failure because you know that any mistakes will guide you to more knowledge, more experience and more ability to deal with any situation.

I believe that hopeful people are buoyant, more upbeat and enthusiastic.

I find that people who I meet who see the glass half full, and not half empty, are more resilient, persistent, engaged and better at recovering from adversity.

The example of a hopeful person in my life and who instilled in me my joy of life, and making the most of every moment, is my mum. For me, she is the definition of being hopeful. My mum suffered tragedy in her life, as I have alluded to in previous chapters. Her parents died young. Her husband, my biological dad died very young at age 30. Her son, my brother, died at age 18.

Now, you might think that my mum would be bitter and resentful, full of woe and questioning why her. However, not once in her life has any of that applied to her. Instead, she always saw possibility and that there would be a positive outcome.

I remember when my brother died, his friends came to see us every Thursday night for a year after his death. They spent the evening remembering Leslie, speaking of their days, and sharing their lives before he died and after. It was an incredible gift to us that they showed their love, and care for Leslie, and us. Also, it was good for them to be able to grieve with us, laugh with us, and put some sort of reason to our loss.

Those friends gave us hope in the darkness that losing Leslie's light had plunged us into. My mum during those nights gave these friends purpose to their lives after their loss. And they in turn gave us strength and inspiration to go forward.

Many of my communication coaching clients are women in a male-dominated work environment. These remarkable women who have achieved so much in their careers, are still the recipients of inequality and prejudice, even in the 21st century! But what these women all have in common is that they are hopeful. They see meaning in their work. They see purpose to their lives, in their work and their relationships.

With this strong sense of meaning and purpose, these women see the bigger picture. They do not give up when faced with the obstacles thrown in front of them. Even when discouraged and facing setbacks, they can see that they can make changes without giving in. They have fuel to work towards something better. They are persistent and always willing to consider other paths if the one they have taken is blocked.

Your actions can spark hope if you feel discouraged, low and without motivation. You can activate feelings of hopefulness by engaging in an activity which is pleasant and/or gets you moving. For me, being by the sea and looking at the waves, lifts my mood. Maybe cooking, or tending to a garden, or sharing a coffee with friends or a tasty meal, can provide hope for you. By being active, you will see that the negative will pass and is not permanent.

Practising hope and being hopeful is so important when you feel that there are insurmountable obstacles before you. Think of famous people in history or today, who overcame all odds by keeping hope alive. For example, Nelson Mandela, Mother Teresa and Martin Luther King. These people not only stayed hopeful, but they worked in communities to bring about the change they wanted to see.

Like those amazing people, you, too, can be hopeful by visioning what you want, collaborate with other people, and practise patience. Keep your conviction that something better is possible for you and for us all.

**Being Hopeful Affirmations**

I recognise that I have options, even when I am in a difficult situation.

I know that this challenge is temporary.

Sunshine after rain, and rainbows after the rain, remind me that there is always hope.

I embrace hope, which fills me with positivity, confidence and trust.

I am empowered by hope.

I am hopeful.

I am being hopeful.

## Chapter 16

# BEING PATIENT

*"Dear Patience"*
*Sung by Niall Horan*

When I was younger, I wanted all my dreams, wishes and goals to be fulfilled immediately. I was prepared to work for them, but I wanted the results. I wanted whatever I thought essential to my life to be there and then. I pushed and pushed, often against brick walls, thinking that my pushing would break them down and I would get what I wanted.

In love, I wanted my beloved to be with me all the time. I could not stand it when she was away from me. In my work, I wanted my achievements to be recognised and valued. In life generally, I was determined and driven. Most of all, I think of myself pushing. Why could it not be now? Why could I not have that purchase now? Why could I not have that role now?

As I became older, I realised that all the pushing in the world did not change the outcome. Indeed, it was a waste of time and energy. If it was right and meant to be, it would be. All that time and energy I wasted in frustration, and anger and feeling out of control.

And this impatience applied to my actions with other people too. Was I understanding and tolerant of my dad when he began his dementia? Not entirely. Was I calm and did I listen, when my mum or elder relatives gave me advice? Did I truly listen, or did I have my mind on the next step that I wanted to take regardless of the practicalities involved?

I was told that, 'Patience is a virtue.' As a younger person, I could not see the sense in that. Now, I realise that we can control our responses and take control of our lives by letting life unfold, and take the direction that we need to go in.

I do not mean that you do not plan, dream, or have goals to work towards, but accept that if a door is being closed on you, it is because a window is going to open. That the door you are banging against will not open unless it is the best door for you to walk through. Have patience that whatever you want to achieve will happen, in good time, and the best time for you. Maybe that is not today, tomorrow, or next week. Maybe it is next year. Whenever it happens, it will be because of your efforts, taking account of the opportunities presented to you and your learning from all the steps taken along the way.

Sometimes being impatient can be a good thing. It can help you to be active and not procrastinate. But mostly, it will lead you to make hasty decisions, agitation when things do not happen as fast as you would like and disappointment because of unrealistic expectations.

However, patience is not to be used as a negative. It is not to hold you back or make you fearful of making changes and accept less than you deserve. Use patience for good reason – when you feel anger, irritation, annoyance, frustration. For example, do not send that email response. Sleep on it. Don't send that proposal yet. Don't send that message. Consider, and take a moment.

Being patient will help you to regulate your emotions, your responses and take control of your actions and decisions. It will reduce stress and enable you to slow down and prioritise your wellbeing.

Part of being patient is being flexible. If you are patient but not flexible, you may find yourself waiting for things to go back to how you originally wanted them. That does not always happen. Plus, waiting too long can mean that you miss opportunities. Flexibility allows you to adapt your goals to be achievable and still bring you success.

When things do not go as planned, be adaptable too.

I think about how much calmer and more peaceful my life is now that I realise what it means to be patient. That

I do not kick against those barriers, unless it is helping me to develop resilience and persistence. Accepting that being patient will lead me into more fulfilling relationships and more rational, realistic decisions.

I know that this day and age promotes instant gratification and instant results but take your time. Reframe errors as a learning opportunity. Trust in yourself that you will reach the heights that you want to climb, and do so slowly and surely, and by being patient.

*"Patience is key to joy."*
*Rumi*

## Being Patient Affirmations

I choose patience because I can then think rationally.

I keep my cool.

Every annoyance and every stressor helps me to practise and master the skill of patience.

I am flexible.

I lovingly trust the process of life.

I am patient.

I am being patient.

Chapter 17

# BEING GRATEFUL

*"Grateful"*
*Sung by Rita Ora*

I began this book by telling the story of how *BEING* came to be, with my friends Linda and Ems, we thought of the word for the year ahead for each of us. One of the words that Linda and I thought of was "Gratitude". Being grateful for everything in our lives.

An unknown author wrote, *'There is always, always, always something to be thankful for.'* I wonder how often you take the time to consider all that you have in your life, rather than all you want?

It is so easy to be always searching, acquiring things, looking for more. Thinking about tomorrow, rather than enjoying today. Thinking that we never have enough.

When we stop and take a moment to think of all we have, and all the people who bring us joy, and support us and care for us, give us love and nourish us, we are immediately happier, less stressed and more contented.

There is a popular saying, 'Count your blessings,' and when you practise that, you realise how much there is in your life that gives you peace and happiness.

Take a moment to list five aspects of your life that are blessings.

For me, those five are: my beloved; the place where I live; that I love my work; that I have dear and wonderful friends and family; and that I am healthy to be able to do my work and write this book.

What are yours?

This short exercise alone starts you thinking about the things that you are grateful for, and it will lead you to think of several more. Every day and every night, I give thanks for things that have happened that day, or things that happen generally in my life – that I have helped someone by my teaching and training and that I have the opportunity to do that because of my work. That I live somewhere that is beautiful, peaceful and safe.

Why not at the end of every day, think of two aspects of your life, which you appreciate, and you are grateful for that day? It can be small things, or big, including that: the train arrived on time; the sun was out; someone smiled at you; or, your boss listened to your ideas and will action them. By thinking of those two things, it will eradicate the strains and stresses of your day.

I ask my students, after I have not seen them for a few days, to tell me and the rest of the class or group, one good thing that has happened for them since we were last together. It is a question that gets them thinking and appreciating that there is something positive happening in their lives. Some people answer that they had a good evening shared with friends, or that they ate a delicious meal, possibly cooked by one of their classmates. Some mention they studied, passed an exam, or gave a successful presentation.

In that moment, we are all sharing gratitude for something positive in our lives, and in that moment, we can feel that there is something good that enriches us and brings joy.

When we are grateful, we take nothing for granted. That we have a safe and secure home, or a loved one to cherish and who cherishes us, that we can eat without being sick or unwell, and that the sun shines on our face, even periodically.

The wonderful thing about being grateful is that it fosters love, kindness and empathy. All the 'beings' that I have written about here are interrelated. For example, being true to yourself leads to being authentic. Being playful leads to being happy. Being kind leads to love. And being loving and being grateful leads to empathy and being connected.

I am so grateful that you have taken the time to read and/or listen to this book. I appreciate that you can see and feel the benefits of 'being' in all the facets I have written about.

## Being Grateful Affirmations

I am grateful for this moment.

I am grateful for endless possibilities.

I give thanks for all the love I have in my life.

I am grateful for all that I have and all that I am.

I take nothing for granted and I am grateful for being alive.

I am grateful.

I am being grateful.

Epilogue

# BEING HERE

*"I'm Still Here (Follies)"*
*Sung by Carol Burnett*

Being here for me is living in a place that I could never have dreamed of being. It is my sanctuary, my haven, where I am at peace and contented. I am eternally grateful that I have the complete pleasure of being here and that it gives me the strength, motivation and inspiration to be.

I deeply appreciate all the people who have been here for me throughout my life. Many of them are no longer with me physically, but their love and support will always be here in my heart and every thought.

I thank everyone for being here with me now and the meaning you give to my life. How you enrich my life and bring me joy.

Being here for you is why I have written this book.

My teaching, training and coaching is to help other people, but this writing, in addition to my first book, is to reach out to you wherever you are in the world, to remind you of the ways of being and not doing. So, you know you always have my support, and encouragement to be wonderful **you**.

# Contact The Author

If this book has touched your heart, helped you, resonated, and you want to contact the author, please go to any of the following platforms.

**LinkedIn:**
https://www.linkedin.com/Alicia Sedgwick - communication coach

**YouTube Channel:**
https://youtube.com/@aliciasedgwick9329

**Facebook:**
https://www.facebook.com/aliciasedgwickcommunicationscoach

**Instagram:**
https://www.instagram.com/aliciasedgwickcommunication

All links to these resources can also be found on the author's website
www.aliciasedgwick.com

# Singer and Song References

**Bruno Mars:** Peter Gene Hernandez; American singer-songwriter, musician, record producer.

**Julie Andrews:** English singer, actress, author. Song written by Oscar Hammerstein and Richard Rodgers.

**Dame Olivia Newton-John:** 1948-2022; English and Australian singer, actress.

**Van Halen:** American rock band formed in Pasadena, California, 1973. Song written in 1991 for their album For Unlawful Carnal Knowledge.

**Rachel Platten:** American singer, songwriter, author.

**Harry Styles:** English singer, songwriter, actor.

**Mary J Blige:** American singer, songwriter, rapper, actress, entrepreneur.

**Nat King Cole:** Nathaniel Adams Coles; 1919-1965; American singer, jazz pianist, actor. Song written by Charles Trenet and recorded several times in France during the 1940s, before Albert Beach penned an English language version.

***The Greatest Showman***: a 2017 American biographical musical drama film directed by Michel Gracey from a screenplay by Jenny Bicks and Bill Condon. The film stars include: Hugh Jackman; Zac Efron; Michelle Williams; Rebecca Ferguson; and Zendaya.

**Pharrell Williams:** Pharrell Lanscilo Williams; American singer, record producer, musician, songwriter, rapper, fashion designer. Song originally recorded by Cee Green, written by Imogen Heap as a commission by Cow & Gate Baby Club to make babies happy!

**Gloria Gaynor:** Gloria Fowles; American singer. Song written by Victor Willis, Henri Belolo, Peter Whitehead and Jacques Morrali, first released by the Village People, 1978 album Macho Man.

**Diana Ross:** American singer, actress, known as the Queen of Motown Records. This song was her first solo single, on her debut album, 1970.

**Jason Upton:** American worship music singer, songwriter and recording artist.

**Cyndi Lauper:** American singer, songwriter, actress. Song originally written and recorded by Robert Hazard.

**Travis Greene:** Travis Montorious Greene; American gospel musician and songwriter.

**Journey:** American rock band formed in San Francisco, 1973.

**Niall James Horan:** Irish singer and songwriter, former member of the boy band, One Direction, formed in 2010 for UK's *X Factor*, singing competition.

**Rita Ora:** Rita Sahatciu Ora; English singer, songwriter, television personality, actress. Song written by Diane Warren, from *Beyond the Lights*, original motion picture soundtrack.

**Carol Burnett:** Carol Creighton Burnett; American singer, comedian and actress. Song written by Stephen Sondheim.

# Quotations and Additional References

**KPMG:** Klynveld Peat Marwick Goerdeler; a multinational professional services network and one of the biggest four accounting organisations in the world. KPMG survey 2020, *Advancing the Future of Women in Business* https://assets.kpmg.com/content/dam/kpmg/sk/pdf/2020/2020-KPMG-Womens-Leadership-Summit-Report.pdf

**Anna Eleanor Roosevelt:** 1884-1962; American political figure, diplomat and activist.

**Jona Laks:** Holocaust survivor, 94, was in Auschwitz aged 12 for more than a year with her twin sister. Reported by CNN Monday January 27, 2025.

**Micro Rainbow:** www.microrainbow.org Non-profit organisation that runs safe houses and socio-economic programmes for LGBTQI+ people fleeing persecution.

*Jewish People's Experiences and Perceptions of Antisemitism:* The European Union Agency for Fundamental Rights (FRA) https://fra.europa.eu/en

**Antony Lishak MBE**: Chief Executive Officer of the Holocaust Education Charity, teacher, author and creative writing expert, creator and curator of *In Their Footsteps* exhibition and educational resource.

**Jenny Stolzenberg:** 1947-2016; visual artist, ceramicist, daughter Holocaust survivor.

**Rupi Kaur:** Canadian poet, illustrator, photographer and Number 1 New York Times bestselling author; *The Sun and Her Flowers*, Andrews McMeel Publishing USA and Simon & Schuster UK, 2017, ISBN 978-1-5011-7526-8.

**Lord Alfred Tennyson:** 1809-1892; 1st Baron Tennyson; English poet and Poet Laureate during much of Queen Victoria's UK reign.

**Sadhguru:** Indian guru, author and founder of the Isha Foundation, based in Coimbatore, India, 1992.

**Merriam-Webster:** American company, publisher of reference books and in particular dictionaries.

**Karl Paul Reinhold Niebuhr:** 1892–1971; American Lutheran theologian, ethicist, commentator about politics and public affairs.

**National Institute of Mental Health in America:** based in Betheseda, Maryland, USA the largest research organisation in the world specialising in mental health.

**Albert Einstein:** 1879-1955; German theoretical physicist best known for developing the Theory of Relativity.

**The Bible:** a collection of religious texts and scriptures, originally written in Hebrew, Aramaic and Koine Greek, held to be sacred in Christianity and partly in Judaism, Samaritanism, Island and the Baha'i Faith, and other Abrahamic religions.

**Robin Hood:** legendary heroic outlaw originally depicted in English folklore and later featured in literature, theatre and cinema.

**Brené Brown:** Casandra Brené Brown; American academic, author, podcaster, researcher and storyteller who spent two decades studying courage, vulnerability, shame and empathy.

**Grace Patricia Kelly:** 1929-1982; also known as Grace of Monaco, was an American actress and Princess of Monaco, as the wife of Prince Rainer 11.

**Morgan Freeman:** American actor, producer and narrator.

**Nelson Mandela:** 1918-2013; South African anti-apartheid activist and politician, who served as the first president of South Africa from 1994-1999.

**Saint Mother Teresa:** Mary Teresa Bojaxhiu; 1910-1997; Albanian Indian Catholic nun.

**Martin Luther King:** 1929-1968; American Baptist minister activist and political philosopher.

**Rumi:** Mohammad Jalâl al-dîn Rûmî, 1207-1273; 13th century Persian poet, Sufi mystic, Islamic scholar and Maruridi theologian.